Sanjeev Kapoor's

MUSHROOM Mania

In association with Alyona Kapoor

Popular Prakashan
www.popularprakashan.com

Published by
POPULAR PRAKASHAN PVT. LTD.
301, Mahalaxmi Chambers
22, Bhulabhai Desai Road
Mumbai - 400 026
for KHANA KHAZANA PUBLICATIONS PVT. LTD.

First Published 2009
Second Reprint August 2014

(4284)
ISBN: 978-81-7991-536-3

Cover Design: Mahendra Ghanekar
Design: Anjali Sawant
Photography: Bharat Bhirangi

PRINTED IN INDIA
by Saurabh Printers Pvt. Ltd.
A-16, Sector 4, Noida

AUTHOR'S NOTE

It is neither a vegetable nor a fruit, nor a kind of meat, but it has been prized as food since ancient times. Mushrooms occupy a class all their own. They are fungi and are considered by many vegetarians as not quite belonging to the plant kingdom! Mushrooms have however, been eaten by people since ancient times, especially in China, Greece and Italy.

The edible part of the mushroom is the fruiting body that grows on a stalk and has a cap and gills on the underside.

There are 38,000 different varieties of mushroom, of which 1,841 are edible. Some species are mildly poisonous which is why eating wild mushrooms is not advisable. The outrageously expensive truffle is also a species of edible fungus that grows under the ground near the roots of old oak trees.

The most popular variety of edible mushrooms, Portobello, are known as button mushrooms when they are young and unopened. Button mushrooms are available fresh, frozen or canned. They have a mild flavour if eaten raw, but are better cooked.

An immature Portobello is known as Crimini or Italian brown because of its earthy brown colour. A full-grown Portobello is as large and brown as a burger bun. It is also called champignon, French for mushroom.

Much sought-after and therefore expensive, are porcino (plural porcini) and morel mushrooms. Porcini have a meaty texture and flavour and a distinctive squat shape. Morels are conical and have a honeycombed surface. These yellow, white and grey mushrooms are ideal for stuffing and for adding piquancy to sauces and stews. Thouands of mushroom hunters in Europe and the U.S.A. fan out into the forests every year to gather morels, which grow under trees.

Japanese shiitake are cultivated on oak logs and are best had in soups and stir-fries. Enoki, another Japanese mushroom with a fruity taste, resembles sprouts with long, thin stems and tiny caps. They are eaten raw in salads. Oyster mushrooms, which resemble an oyster and even taste like one, are yet another Oriental favourite.

And finally, there is one mushroom that looks entirely unlike the others. Trumpet-shaped and yellow-gold in color, Chanterelle or Girolle mushrooms have a rich flavour that ranges from apricot to peppery.

Mushrooms are high in fibre and low in calories, free of fat and bad cholesterol and very low in sodium. They provide several nutrients including thiamine, biotin, ascorbic acid, riboflavin, niacin and some minerals like selenium, iron, potassium and phosphorus.

Here are some tips for buying, storing, cleaning and cooking mushrooms.

Buying and Storing

- Mushrooms are best bought fresh, but they also taste good dried. They should not have dark spots or holes.
- Store fresh mushrooms in a refrigerator in paper bags or wrapped in paper towels, never in plastic.
- Store dried mushrooms in an airtight container in a cool, dry place.
- If you want to freeze fresh mushroms, clean them thoroughly. Then slice them if they are big, or keep them whole if they are small. To retain the colour, dip the whole mushrooms or mushroom slices in a solution of lemon juice and water for five minutes.
- You can either steam them or fry them before freezing. Steamed mushrooms keep longer. Steam whole mushrooms 5 minutes, buttons or quarters 3½ minutes and slices 3 minutes. Cool immediately, drain and pack them in containers lined with wax paper, or in plastic bags,leaving ½-inch headspace. Seal and freeze.
- Or heat small quantities of mushrooms in butter, margarine or olive oil in an open frying pan until almost done. Cool completely. Pack into containers or plastic bags, leaving ½-inch head space. Seal and freeze. Never directly freeze a bag of fresh mushrooms.

Cleaning

- Do not prepare mushrooms until just before using. There is no need to peel the mushrooms. Trim the stalks and sprinkle a little refined flour over them. Lightly rub the mushrooms and rinse under running water. Pat dry and then use as required. Mushrooms are easily saturated with water and tend to become mushy if soaked. Use a soft brush to clean sand, grit and other debris from the pits and ridges. To reconstitute dried mushrooms, soak in hot water or chicken broth for approximately thirty minutes. Use a fine sieve lined with paper towels or cheese cloth to drain the liquid from the mushrooms. Reserve the liquid as stock for soups and sauces. If there is sand or grit still remaining, rinse and drain the mushrooms again. If the dried mushrooms are going to be added to a soup, they do not need to be reconstituted first.

- The stems of varieties like Portobello and Shiitake are tough and must be removed, but they can be used to flavour certain dishes.

Cooking

Mushrooms must always be cooked as they may contain toxins, which can upset the stomach. The best way of cooking mushrooms is to sauté in a little butter or oil on high heat. They cook fast and should never be overcooked as they turn black. If you cook them on low heat they start sweating moisture and turn black more quickly. Mushrooms can also be broiled, fried, or eaten raw. Wild mushrooms require longer cooking time than cultivated mushrooms. Aluminium pans tend to turn mushrooms black, so avoid using this type of pan when cooking.

I have collected some delicious mushroom recipes in this book just for you! Try the interesting Mushroom and Paneer Clear Soup, crunchy Grilled Chicken and Mushroom Salad, crispy Phal-Subz Seekh and scrumptious Cheesy Mushrooms. Relish silky Mushroom Quiche and rich Shahi Dhingri Matar Paneer or tuck into filling Rice with Stewed Mushrooms and Chicken and spicy Gobhi Mushroom Chilli Fry.

Each recipe is meant for four portions when it is a part of a menu with other complementary dishes.

Happy Cooking!

CONTENTS

SOUPS, SALADS AND SNACKS

MAIN COURSE

Mushroom and Paneer Clear Soup

Ingredients

6 fresh button mushrooms, sliced

150 grams cottage cheese, grated

½ tablespoon refined flour

1 teaspoon oil + for deep-frying

2 spring onions, chopped

2 garlic cloves, chopped

4-5 cups Vegetable Stock (see below)

salt to taste

½ tablespoon soy sauce

¼ teaspoon MSG (optional)

1 celery stalk, chopped

8-10 black peppercorns, crushed

¼ cup blanched vermicelli

1½ teaspoons lemon juice

4-5 fresh basil leaves

Method

1. Mix the grated cottage cheese with refined flour and knead into a smooth dough. Divide into eight equal portions and shape into balls. Heat the oil in a *kadai* and deep-fry till light golden. Drain on absorbent paper.
2. Heat one teaspoon of oil in a wok; add the spring onions and garlic and sauté

over medium heat for half a minute. Add the mushrooms and continue to sauté for another minute.

3. Add the vegetable stock and bring to a boil.
4. Add the salt, soy sauce, MSG, celery and crushed peppercorns. Simmer, uncovered, for four to five minutes.
5. Stir in the vermicelli and fried cottage cheese balls and lemon juice.
6. Ladle immediately into individual soup bowls and serve hot, garnished with roughly-torn basil leaves.

Vegetable Stock

Peel, wash and chop 1 onion, ½ medium carrot, 2-3 inch celery stalk and 2-3 garlic cloves. Place in a pan with 1 bay leaf, 5-6 peppercorns, 2-3 cloves and five cups of water and bring to a boil. Lower heat and simmer for fifteen minutes and strain. Cool and store in a refrigerator till further use.

Mushroom Soup

Ingredients

200 grams fresh mushrooms

2 medium onions, roughly chopped

300 ml milk

2 bay leaves

5-6 peppercorns

4 cloves

2 tablespoons butter

1 tablespoon refined flour

¾ cup fresh cream

salt to taste

½ teaspoon white pepper powder

a pinch of nutmeg powder

Method

1. Slice four to five mushrooms and roughly chop the remaining.
2. Boil the milk along with bay leaves, peppercorns and cloves. Strain and keep the milk hot.
3. In a pan, heat the butter. and add the onions and chopped mushrooms and cook till they are soft. Add the flour and sauté till the raw flavour disappears, taking care that the flour does not get burnt.
4. Pour the milk into the pan slowly and stir continuously to prevent lumps from

forming. Cook for five minutes. Purée the mixture when a little cold; the soup should have a smooth texture and the consistency should not be thin.

5. Bring to a boil and correct the consistency by adding more milk if required. Add the cream, reserving a little for garnishing, salt, pepper powder and nutmeg powder. Stir well.
6. Serve hot, garnished with reserved mushroom slices and cream.

Chef's Tip

Use raw sliced mushrooms for garnishing. However, if you wish, you may sauté them in a little butter or oil and then use.

Mushroom Cappuccino

Ingredients

15 large fresh button mushrooms, thickly sliced

1 tablespoon butter

1 bay leaf

1 small onion, chopped

4-6 garlic cloves, chopped

4 cups Vegetable Stock (page 10)

salt to taste

¼ teaspoon white pepper powder

¾ cup cream

2 cups milk, chilled

1 teaspoon cinnamon powder

Method

1. Melt the butter in a heavy-bottomed pan. Add the bay leaf, onion and garlic and sauté for two to three minutes or till onion is translucent.
2. Add the mushrooms and sauté for one minute. Add one cup of vegetable stock and cook for five more minutes. Remove from heat and cool. Remove the bay leaf and discard.
3. Make a purée of the cooked mushrooms and add the remaining vegetable stock. Return to heat and bring to a boil. Add the salt and white pepper powder, lower heat and simmer for two to three minutes.

4. Stir in the cream and remove from heat. Pour the soup into individual cups and keep warm.
5. Pour the chilled milk into a chilled bowl. Beat with a fork till it develops a thick froth. Collect the froth with a ladle and place on the hot mushroom soup giving it a cappuccino effect.
6. Sprinkle cinnamon powder and serve immediately.

Chef's Tip
Use milk with a high-fat content for a thick froth.

Mushroom Soup with Chillies

Ingredients

20-25 fresh button mushrooms, quartered

4 cups Vegetable Stock (page 10)

1 tablespoon oil

salt to taste

1 inch ginger, cut into strips

¼ cup chopped fresh coriander

4-5 stalks spring onion greens, chopped

Chilli paste

1 tablespoon oil

4 dried red chillies, halved

4 shallots, chopped

3 garlic cloves, chopped

1 inch galangal, sliced

Method

1. For the chilli paste, heat the oil in a pan; add the dried chillies, shallots, garlic and galangal and sauté for four to five minutes. Cool and grind to a fine paste.
2. For the soup, heat one tablespoon of oil in a separate pan; add the mushrooms and sauté for one minute. Transfer the mushrooms to a plate.
3. To the same pan, add the vegetable stock and bring to a boil.

4. Add the salt, sautéed mushrooms and ginger strips. Stir in the chilli paste and simmer for five minutes.
5. Sprinkle fresh coriander and spring onion greens over the soup and serve hot.

Zuppa Di Funghi

Ingredients

5-6 dried chanterelle mushrooms, soaked and cut into strips

25-30 fresh button mushrooms, sliced

6 tablespoons butter

5 garlic cloves, chopped

2 medium onions, sliced

2 tablespoons refined flour

5 cups Vegetable Stock (page 10)

½ teaspoon mixed dried herbs

salt to taste

5-6 black peppercorns, freshly ground

Method

1. Heat one tablespoon of butter in a pan and add the dried mushrooms strips. Sauté gently over low heat for five minutes. Remove the mushrooms and set aside.
2. Add three tablespoons of butter to the same pan. Add the garlic and onions and sauté for two minutes without browning. Add the button mushrooms and continue to sauté for five more minutes.
3. In a separate pan, heat two tablespoons of butter; add flour and sauté for two minutes. Add the vegetable stock and

stir continuously for two minutes so that no lumps form.

4. Add the mushroom-onion mixture and simmer for another five minutes over very low heat. Season with dried herbs, salt and freshly ground peppercorns. Set aside to cool.
5. Purée the mixture in a food processor or blender and strain the purée into a clean pan. Add more stock if the purée is too thick and adjust seasoning. Bring the soup to a boil again. Serve hot, garnished with the sautéed dried mushrooms.

Chef's Tip

Use any dried mushrooms if chanterelle mushrooms are not available.

Mushroom Soup with Light Soy Sauce

Ingredients

30 grams fresh button mushrooms

1 teaspoon light soy sauce

3 cups Vegetable Stock (page 10)

150 grams silken tofu, finely diced

salt to taste

½ teaspoon black pepper powder

4 teaspoons sliced spring onions

Method

1. Pour the vegetable stock and light soy sauce in a deep pan and bring the mixture to a boil.
2. Add the mushrooms and tofu and cook over low heat for three to four minutes, but do not allow the mixture to boil. Add the salt and pepper powder. Stir to mix well.
3. Ladle into individual soup bowls, sprinkle a teaspoon of spring onions on top and serve piping hot.

Mushroom Soup with Light Soy Sauce

Minted Mushrooms

Ingredients

1 cup fresh mint

400 grams mushrooms, quartered

2 tablespoons lemon juice

salt to taste

1 medium cucumber, peeled and cut into ½-inch pieces

1 medium tomato, seeded and cut into ½-inch pieces

3 tablespoons skimmed milk yogurt

4-5 cabbage or lettuce leaves

Method

1. Place the mushrooms in a thick-bottomed vessel along with the lemon juice and a little salt. Stew them over low heat for ten minutes. Set aside.
2. Chop the mint leaves, reserving one or two sprigs for garnishing.
3. Combine the mushrooms, cucumber, tomato and chopped mint. Mix in the yogurt and salt and toss lightly.
4. Serve on a bed of cabbage leaves or lettuce leaves garnished with a sprig of mint leaves.

Mushroom and Cheese Salad

Ingredients

10-12 fresh button mushrooms, quartered

100 grams processed cheese, cut into small cubes

4 large lettuce leaves, roughly torn

2 garlic cloves, chopped

3 tablespoons Vinaigrette (see alongside)

1 tablespoon chopped fresh coriander

Method

1. Place the mushrooms, cheese, lettuce and garlic in a bowl.
2. Pour the vinaigrette over and toss to mix. Place in a refrigerator for twenty minutes. Garnish with fresh coriander and serve.

Vinaigrette

In a glass jar, combine ½ cup olive oil, 2 tablespoons vinegar, 1 teaspoon mustard paste, 6-8 crushed black peppercorns and salt to taste. Close tightly with the lid and shake well to mix.

Mushroom Salad

Ingredients

10-12 fresh button mushrooms, quartered

10-12 cherry tomatoes

1 small head iceberg lettuce, roughly torn

1 small orange, peeled and segmented

2-3 tablespoons orange juice

2 teaspoons olive oil

salt to taste

1 tablespoon black peppercorns, freshly ground

Method

1. Place the button mushrooms in a bowl. Add the cherry tomatoes, lettuce, orange, orange juice, olive oil, salt and black peppercorns and toss well.
2. Serve chilled.

Chef's Tip
Place the lettuce in ice cold water so as to keep it crisp and fresh.

Grilled Chicken and Mushroom Salad

Ingredients

2 (150 grams each) boneless chicken breasts

6 large fresh button mushrooms, sliced thickly

salt to taste

½ teaspoon black pepper powder

½ teaspoon mustard paste

½ teaspoon garlic paste

2 tablespoons oil

1 medium yellow capsicum

1 medium red capsicum

6 black olives, stoned and sliced

½ head iceberg lettuce, roughly torn

Dressing

1 tablespoon olive oil

1½ tablespoons lemon juice

7-8 black peppercorns, crushed

2 teaspoons powdered sugar

salt to taste

Method

1. Marinate the chicken breasts in salt, pepper powder, mustard paste and garlic paste for twenty minutes.
2. Mix together all the ingredients for the dressing.
3. Grill the chicken breasts for ten to twelve minutes. Cool, slice and set aside.
4. Brush the mushrooms with oil and grill for two minutes. Cut into quarters and set aside.
5. Brush the yellow and red capsicums with oil and grill for ten minutes, turning them once or twice to cook evenly. Cut in half, remove the seeds, slice and set aside.
6. Place the chicken, mushrooms, capsicums, olives and lettuce in a large bowl.
7. Pour the dressing over the salad and toss well to mix. Serve immediately.

Mushrooms in Balsamic Vinegar

Ingredients

400 grams fresh button mushrooms, quartered

2 teaspoons balsamic vinegar

salt to taste

2 teaspoons garlic paste

5-6 fresh basil leaves, torn

5 tablespoons sugar

½ teaspoon black peppercorns, crushed

Method

1. Marinate the mushrooms in a mixture of salt, garlic paste and basil leaves for two hours.
2. Heat the sugar in a pan. Add one tablespoon of water and stir continuously till it caramalizes to a light golden colour.
3. Add the balsamic vinegar and crushed peppercorns and cook for three to four minutes.
4. Toss the mushrooms in the caramelized sugar mixture and keep in a refrigerator to chill. Serve chilled.

Mushrooms in Balsamic Vinegar

Cheesy Mushrooms

Ingredients

16 medium fresh button mushrooms

¼ cup crumbled cottage cheese

¼ cup grated processed cheese

1 medium onion, finely chopped

4-5 garlic cloves, finely chopped

¼ teaspoon white pepper powder

¼ teaspoon nutmeg powder

salt to taste

5 tablespoons butter

1 tablespoon lemon juice

Method

1. Remove the stalks of the mushrooms and chop them finely.
2. Place the chopped mushroom stalks, onion, garlic, cottage cheese, processed cheese, white pepper powder, nutmeg powder and salt in a microwave-safe dish. Add two tablespoons of butter and mix well. Cook, uncovered, on HIGH (100%) for six minutes.
3. Stuff the mushroom caps with the mixture; sandwich two caps together, holding them in place with a toothpick.
4. Brush the remaining butter and lemon juice over the mushrooms and cook, uncovered, on MEDIUM (70%) for three minutes. Serve hot with a spicy sauce.

Mushroom and Paneer Kababs

Ingredients

14-16 button mushrooms

200 grams cottage cheese, cut into 1½-inch cubes

18-20 cherry tomatoes

2 large capsicums, seeded and cut into 1-inch pieces

3 medium onions, cut into 1-inch pieces

2 inches ginger

8-10 garlic cloves

2-3 green chillies, seeded and roughly chopped

2 teaspoons oil

1 teaspoon red chilli flakes

2 teaspoons honey

1 teaspoon cumin powder

1 teaspoon *garam masala* powder

salt to taste

2 teaspoons lemon juice

1 teaspoon *chaat masala*

Method

1. Grind the ginger, garlic and green chillies to a paste
2. In a bowl, mix together the oil, ginger-garlic-green chilli paste, chilli flakes, honey, cumin powder, *garam masala*

powder, salt, lemon juice and *chaat masala*.

3. Marinate the cottage cheese, button mushrooms, cherry tomatoes, capsicums and onions in the mixture for about an hour.
4. Soak eight-inch long wooden satay sticks or skewers in water for half an hour. Remove from the water and thread the marinated cottage cheese cubes, mushrooms, cherry tomatoes, capsicum and onion pieces one after the other onto the sticks or skewers.
5. Cook on an open charcoal fire or directly over a gas flame for five minutes, rotating the stick for even cooking. Alternately cook in a preheated oven for about fifteen minutes.
6. Serve hot.

Chef's Tip

The wooden skewers are soaked in water to prevent them from burning while cooking. This is particularly necessary while grilling or cooking over an open flame.

Phal-Subz Seekh

Ingredients

2 unripe bananas

2 medium potatoes, boiled and mashed

200 grams fresh button mushrooms, chopped

1 small carrot, grated

4 broccoli florets, chopped

1½ tablespoons butter

¾ teaspoon carom seeds

¾ tablespoon chopped fresh coriander

¾ inch ginger, chopped

1½ fresh red chillies, chopped

salt to taste

12 prunes, stoned and chopped

½ teaspoon black salt

¾ teaspoon black pepper powder

½ teaspoon green cardamom powder

a pinch of sandalwood powder

a pinch of dried rose petal powder

½ cup breadcrumbs

1½ tablespoons oil

Method

1. Boil, cool, peel and grate the bananas.
2. Heat the butter in a pan; add the carom seeds and sauté over medium heat for ten seconds. Add the potatoes, mushrooms, carrots and broccoli and sauté till the moisture evaporates. Add the fresh

coriander, ginger, red chillies and salt. Stir and remove from heat and set aside to cool.

3. Place the cooled mixture in a blender with the grated bananas, prunes, black salt, pepper powder, cardamom powder, sandalwood powder, rose petal powder, and breadcrumbs and process till smooth.
4. Transfer the mixture to a bowl and divide into equal portions. Pat the mixture onto skewers into four-inch long *seekh kababs.*
5. Preheat a *tandoor*. Cook the *kababs* in the *tandoor* for six or seven minutes, basting occasionally with oil.
6. Alternatively, shape each portion into a croquette, arrange on a greased baking tray and grill in a preheated oven at 180ºC/350ºF/Gas Mark 4 for six or seven minutes.
7. Arrange the *kababs* on a platter and serve hot with Kachumber (see below).

Kachumber

Cut 1 medium tomato, 1 medium cucumber, 1 medium green capsicum, ½ medium white radish and 1 medium carrot, into ½-inch pieces. Mix the vegetables in a bowl and add 1 medium onion chopped, 2 chopped green chillies, 2 tablespoons chopped fresh coriander, 1 tablespoon lemon juice and salt to taste. Toss well. Transfer to a salad bowl and serve cold.

Phal-Subz Seekh

Mushroom and Spinach Pancakes

Ingredients

100 grams fresh mushrooms, chopped

2 medium bunches (600 grams) spinach leaves, roughly chopped

¾ cup wholewheat flour

1 teaspoon oil

6-8 garlic cloves, chopped

1 medium onion, chopped

salt to taste

¼ teaspoon white pepper powder

¾ cup skimmed milk

¼ teaspoon carom seeds

Method

1. For the filling, heat the oil in a pan, add the garlic and stir-fry briefly. Add the onion and chopped mushrooms and cook till the onion becomes soft and translucent. Cook on high heat so that the excess moisture from the onions and mushrooms dries up.
2. Add the spinach, salt and white pepper powder, and cook until all the moisture evaporates. Remove from the heat and divide the spinach mixture into eight equal portions and keep warm.
3. For the batter, mix the salt with the flour and add milk. Whisk well. Add water as

required, to make a smooth batter of pouring consistency. Strain the batter if there are lumps.

4. Add the carom seeds and stir well. Rest the batter for at least fifteen minutes.
5. Heat a six-inch non-stick pan. Grease with a little oil. Pour half a ladle of batter and spread into a round shape. Cook for half a minute on medium heat, turn over and cook slightly.
6. Spread a portion of the cooked spinach on three-fourth of the pancake and roll it ensuring that the filling does not spill out.
7. Cook the rest of the pancakes in a similar way. Serve immediately.

Mushroom, Babycorn and Paneer Tawa Masala

Ingredients

8-10 fresh button mushrooms, halved

8-10 babycorn cobs, halved and boiled

400 grams cottage cheese, cut into 1½-inch cubes

10 baby potatoes, parboiled

10-15 shallots

5 teaspoons + 3 tablespoons oil

2 large onions, chopped

1½ inches ginger, chopped

3-4 green chillies, chopped

½ teaspoon coriander powder

½ teaspoon red chilli powder

4 teaspoons *garam masala* powder

salt to taste

8 tablespoons tomato purée

1 tablespoon lemon juice

2 tablespoons chopped fresh coriander

Method

1. Sauté the mushrooms, babycorn cobs, cottage cheese, baby potatoes and shallots separately in one teaspoon of oil each, sprinkling a little salt as you sauté. Drain on absorbent paper and set aside.
2. Heat three tablespoons of oil on a *tawa*; add the onions and sauté till brown. Add the ginger and continue to sauté.

Add a little water and cook for a few minutes.

3. Place the sautéed cottage cheese and vegetables around the edge of the *tawa*.
4. Add the green chillies to the onion mixture and continue to sauté.
5. Draw the vegetables and cottage cheese into the *masala* at the centre of the *tawa*. Add the coriander powder, chilli powder, *garam masala* powder, salt, tomato purée and half a cup of water and mix well. Cook for three to four minutes, then add the lemon juice and mix.
6. Garnish with the fresh coriander and serve hot.

Mushroom Soyawadi Masala

Ingredients

15-20 fresh mushrooms, quartered

1½ cups soya bean *wadi*

1½ teaspoon oil

1 bay leaf

½ teaspoon peppercorns, crushed

1 inch ginger, chopped

5 garlic cloves, chopped

3 medium onions, chopped

1 teaspoon red chilli powder

1 teaspoon coriander powder

¼ teaspoon turmeric powder

2 medium tomatoes, chopped finely

salt to taste

½ teaspoon *garam masala* powder

a few sprigs of fresh mint, chopped

Method

1. Soak the soya bean *wadi* in warm water for 15-20 minutes. Squeeze and remove excess water, cut into two and set aside.
2. Heat the oil in a non-stick pan, add the bay leaf, crushed peppercorns and stir-fry briefly.
3. Add the chopped ginger and garlic and cook on high heat for half a minute, stirring continuously.

4. Add the onions and continue cooking till the onions turn translucent.
5. Add the chilli powder, coriander powder and turmeric powder and stir well. Mix in the tomatoes, add salt and continue cooking over medium heat.
6. Add the mushrooms and soaked soya bean *wadi*. Stir well.
7. Sprinkle the *garam masala* powder, fresh mint and salt. Mix well. Cook over high heat for two minutes. Cover and simmer over medium heat for two-three minutes.

Mushroom Balchao

Ingredients

600 grams fresh button mushrooms, quartered

10-12 dried red chillies

8-10 garlic cloves

1 inch ginger

1 teaspoon cumin seeds

7-8 cloves

1 teaspoon mustard seeds

1 inch cinnamon

salt to taste

½ cup malt vinegar

2 tablespoons oil

2 medium onions, chopped

2 medium tomatoes, chopped

¾ cup tomato purée

1 tablespoon sugar

Method

1. Grind together the red chillies, garlic, ginger, cumin seeds, cloves, mustard seeds, cinnamon and salt with one-fourth cup of malt vinegar to a fine paste.
2. Heat the oil in a *kadai*; add the onions and sauté till light brown. Add the tomatoes, mix well and cook for five minutes, stirring continuously.

3. Add the mushrooms, tomato purée and ground *masala* and cook for three or four minutes. Add the sugar, more salt if necessary and mix well.
4. Add the remaining malt vinegar and cook for five to seven minutes.
5. Serve hot.

Masala Khumb

Ingredients

600 grams fresh button mushrooms, quartered

8 dried red chillies

3 teaspoons coriander seeds

1 tablespoon oil

1 teaspoon cumin seeds

2 medium onions, sliced

3 teaspoons garlic paste

4 large tomatoes, puréed

salt to taste

4 green chillies, chopped

2 inches ginger, chopped

2 teaspoons *garam masala* powder

½ cup chopped fresh coriander

Method

1. Roast and pound the dried red chillies and coriander seeds with a mortar and pestle to a coarse powder.
2. Heat the oil in a *kadai*. Add the cumin seeds, onions and garlic paste and sauté for one minute over medium heat. Add the powdered spices and sauté for half a minute.
3. Add the tomato purée and salt and sauté till the oil separates. Add the green chillies and ginger and continue to sauté for one minute. Add the mushrooms and salt and cook, stirring gently, for seven to eight minutes. Stir in the *garam masala* powder. Garnish with fresh coriander and serve hot with *roti*.

Khumb Hara Dhania

Ingredients

600 grams fresh button mushrooms, trimmed

1 cup chopped fresh coriander

2 tablespoons oil

5 green cardamoms

1 black cardamom

5 cloves

1 inch cinnamon

1 bay leaf

a pinch of mace

$^{2}/_{3}$ cup boiled onion paste

4 teaspoons ginger paste

4 teaspoons garlic paste

4 green chillies, chopped

1 teaspoon red chilli powder

½ teaspoon coriander powder

1½ cups yogurt, whisked

salt to taste

3 tablespoons cashew nut paste

1½ inches ginger, cut into thin strips

Method

1. Blanch the mushrooms in hot water for two minutes. Drain.
2. Heat the oil in a *kadai*; add the green and black cardamoms, cloves, cinnamon,

bay leaf and mace and sauté over medium heat till fragrant.

3. Add the boiled onion paste and sauté for two or three minutes. Add the ginger and garlic pastes and continue to sauté for a while. Add the green chillies and sauté for half a minute.
4. Add the chilli powder and coriander powder and stir for half a minute.
5. Remove from heat and stir in the yogurt and salt. Return the pan to the heat. Add around three-fourth cup of water and bring to a boil. Lower heat and simmer till the oil rises to the surface. Add the cashew nut paste and simmer for two or three minutes.
6. Add the mushrooms and three-fourth cup of fresh coriander and simmer for two or three minutes. Transfer to a serving dish and garnish with the remaining fresh coriander and ginger strips.
7. Serve hot with steamed rice or *roti*.

Mashobra Mushroom Curry

Ingredients

20-24 fresh button mushrooms, quartered

2 inches ginger

4-6 garlic cloves

10-12 cashew nuts

1 tablespoon poppy seeds

1 tablespoon melon seeds

4 tablespoons oil

2 medium onions, finely chopped

1 teaspoon red chilli powder

1 teaspoon coriander powder

½ teaspoon cumin powder

salt to taste

2 medium tomatoes, puréed

2 tablespoons yogurt, whisked

½ teaspoon *garam masala* powder

¼ cup fresh coriander, chopped

Method

1. Grind the ginger and garlic to a fine paste.
2. Soak the cashew nuts, poppy seeds and melon seeds in hot water for ten minutes, drain and grind to a fine paste and set aside.
3. Heat the oil in a pan, add the chopped onions and sauté for two to three

minutes or until light brown in colour. Add the ginger-garlic paste and stir-fry briefly.

4. Add the chilli, coriander and cumin powders and salt. Stir well and add the tomato purée. Cook on medium heat, stirring continuously for two minutes or till the oil separates. Add the mushrooms and sauté for two minutes on high heat.
5. Mix the cashew nuts, poppy and melon seed pastes in the yogurt and stir in one-and-a-half cups water. Add to the mushroom mixture. Bring to a boil, reduce heat and simmer for five minutes or until the mushrooms are cooked.
6. Sprinkle the *garam masala* powder and chopped coriander and serve hot.

Chinese Garlic Mushrooms

Ingredients

16-20 garlic cloves

20-24 mushrooms

1 tablespoon lemon juice

1 teaspoon soy sauce

½ teaspoon white pepper powder

¼ teaspoon MSG

salt to taste

¾ cup refined flour

½ cup + 2 tablespoons cornflour

¼ teaspoon baking powder

¾ cup oil + 3 tablespoons + for deep-frying

2-3 whole red chillies, halved

4 tablespoons tomato sauce

1 tablespoon vinegar

2 tablespoons red chilli paste

1 tablespoon hot black bean paste

1 teaspoon sugar

1 cup Vegetable Stock (page 10)

½ medium green capsicum, seeded and cut into ½-inch diamonds

½ medium red capsicum, seeded, and cut into ½-inch diamonds

1 medium onion, quartered and layers separated

1 spring onion, finely sliced

1 tablespoon sesame oil

1 tablespoon red chilli flakes

Method

1. Grind six cloves of garlic to a smooth paste. Chop the rest.
2. Mix the garlic paste, lemon juice, soy sauce, white pepper powder, MSG and salt to taste. Marinate the mushrooms in the mixture for ten to fifteen minutes.
3. Mix the refined flour, half cup cornflour, baking powder, three-fourth cup of oil, salt to taste and three-fourth cup of water. Whisk thoroughly to make a batter of pouring consistency and set aside for twenty minutes.
4. Heat sufficient oil in a wok, dip the marinated mushrooms in the batter and deep-fry for two to three minutes on medium heat, turning frequently or until crisp and golden brown. Drain on absorbent paper and set aside. Mix two tablespoons of cornflour in one cup of water.
5. Heat three tablespoons of oil in a wok, add the whole red chillies and chopped garlic and stir-fry briefly. Add the tomato sauce, vinegar, chilli paste, hot black bean paste, sugar and salt to taste. Stir in the vegetable stock and continue to cook on high heat for a minute.
6. Add the capsicums, onion and spring onion and cook for a couple of minutes more. Stir in the cornflour mixture and cook till it starts to thicken.
7. Add the deep-fried mushrooms and toss well to coat. Drizzle the sesame oil, sprinkle chilli flakes and serve hot.

Khumb Hara Pyaaz

Ingredients

40 (400 grams) fresh button mushrooms, quartered

10-12 spring onions, cut into diagonal pieces

5 spring onion greens, chopped

12 garlic cloves, finely chopped

1 tablespoon rice flour

1 cup skimmed milk yogurt, whisked

3 cloves

3 green chillies, seeded and chopped

2 teaspoons coriander powder

salt to taste

½ teaspoon red chilli powder

1 teaspoon turmeric powder

Method

1. Heat a non-stick pan, add the chopped garlic and roast for a minute. Add the mushrooms and continue cooking for three to four minutes on low heat. Add the rice flour and mix.
2. Stir in the yogurt and cook till it thickens.
3. Add the cloves, spring onions and green chillies and continue to cook on low heat for two minutes.
4. Add the coriander powder, salt, chilli powder, turmeric powder and half a cup of water. Cook for two to three minutes. Sprinkle the spring onions greens. Serve hot.

Khumb Hara Pyaaz

Chicken and Mushroom in Hot Tomato Sauce

Ingredients

500 grams boneless chicken, cut into 1-inch pieces

10-12 mushrooms, quartered

1 large tomato, blanched and cut into 1-inch cubes

¾ cup tomato purée

2 tablespoons butter

3-4 spring onions, roughly chopped

5 garlic cloves, roughly chopped

salt to taste

1 tablespoon crushed red chillies

1½ teaspoons Worcestershire sauce

5-6 black peppercorns, crushed

2 teaspoons honey

¼ teaspoon dried oregano

2-3 spring onion greens, roughly chopped

Method

1. Mix together the butter, spring onions, garlic, chicken and salt in a deep microwave bowl. Cover and cook on Microwave HIGH (100%) for four minutes.
2. Add the tomato, tomato purée, crushed red chillies, Worcestershire sauce, peppercorns and mushrooms. Cover and cook on Microwave HIGH (100%) for three minutes.

3. Add the honey and dried oregano to the tomato gravy, cover and cook on Microwave HIGH (100%) for two minutes.
4. Sprinkle the spring onion greens and serve hot.

Shahi Dhingri Matar Paneer

Ingredients

10-15 fresh button mushrooms, halved

1 cup shelled green peas, boiled

100 grams cottage cheese, cut into ½-inch cubes

oil for deep-frying

2 large onions, sliced

10 cashew nuts

2 tablespoons ghee

3 green cardamoms

1 black cardamom

3 cloves

1 inch cinnamon

6-8 black peppercorns

1 bay leaf

1½ tablespoons *khoya/mawa*, grated

¼ teaspoon turmeric powder

1 teaspoon red chilli powder

½ cup yogurt

2 teaspoons coriander powder

½ teaspoon cumin powder

salt to taste

3 tablespoons fresh cream

1 teaspoon *garam masala* powder

Shahi Dhingri Matar Paneer

Method

1. Heat the oil in a *kadai* and deep-fry the sliced onions till well browned. Cool slightly and grind to a fine paste. Grind the cashew nuts with a little water to a fine paste.
2. Heat the ghee in a pan; add the green cardamoms, black cardamom, cloves, cinnamon, peppercorns and bay leaf. When the spices begin to sizzle, add the mushrooms and sauté for a few minutes.
3. Add the *khoya/mawa* and sauté for two minutes.
4. Add the browned onion paste and cashew nut paste and sauté for a few seconds.
5. Add the turmeric powder and chilli powder and mix well. Stir in the yogurt, mix well and cook for two to three minutes.
6. Add the coriander powder, cumin powder and salt and mix well. Add the boiled peas and cook for three to four minutes.
7. Stir in the fresh cream and cottage cheese cubes and sprinkle with *garam masala* powder. Stir gently and serve hot.

Kachchi Makai Dhingri

Ingredients

10-12 medium fresh button mushrooms, quartered

10-12 fresh babycorn cobs, cut into ½-inch pieces

½ cup sweetcorn kernels

1 medium capsicum, seeded and cut into ½-inch strips

1 inch ginger

6-8 garlic cloves

4 tablespoons oil

2 bay leaves

1 medium onion, grated

2 green chillies, slit

1 tablespoon red chilli powder

2 tablespoons coriander powder

1 teaspoon turmeric powder

½ tablespoon cumin powder

1 medium tomato, finely chopped

salt to taste

¼ cup fresh cream

¼ cup fresh coriander, finely chopped

1 teaspoon *garam masala* powder

Method

1. Grind the ginger and garlic to a fine paste.
2. Heat the oil in a pan, add the bay leaves, grated onion and slit green chillies and sauté for three to four minutes or until the onion turns light brown in colour. Add the ginger-garlic paste and stir-fry briefly.
3. Add the chilli, coriander, turmeric and cumin powders. Mix well and add the chopped tomato. Cook on high heat for two to three minutes, stirring continuously. Add the mushroom, babycorn cobs sweetcorn kernels and salt to taste and continue to cook for five minutes on medium heat.
4. Add the capsicum strips, toss well and cook for three to four minutes on medium heat, stirring continuously. Stir in the fresh cream, sprinkle fresh coriander and *garam masala* powder and serve hot.

Matar Mushroom

Ingredients

1½ cups shelled green peas

200 grams mushrooms, quartered

2 tablespoons oil

4 green cardamoms

1 inch cinnamon

2 large onions, chopped finely

1 tablespoon ginger paste

1 tablespoon garlic paste

½ cup tomato purée

1 tablespoon red chilli powder

1 tablespoon coriander powder

1 teaspoon turmeric powder

1 teaspoon *garam masala* powder

salt to taste

½ cup cashew nut paste

Method

1. Heat the oil in a *kadai*. Add the cardamoms, cinnamon and chopped onions and sauté until light golden brown.
2. Add the ginger and garlic pastes and cook for half a minute. Add the tomato purée, chilli, coriander, turmeric and *garam masala* powders and salt and cook till the oil separates from the *masala*.

3. Add the cashew nut paste mixed in one cup of water and stir well. Add a cup of water, bring to a boil and add the green peas and mushrooms. Cook on high heat for seven to eight minutes or till the green peas are cooked completely.
4. Cook on a low flame for five minutes. Serve hot.

Pan-fried Mushrooms

Ingredients

20-24 fresh button mushrooms, quartered

½ cup porcini mushrooms (optional)

½ cup oyster mushrooms (optional)

1 small red capsicum, cut into ½-inch pieces

1 small yellow capsicum, cut into ½-inch pieces

1 tablespoon olive oil

2 medium onions, cut into ½-inch cubes

3 garlic cloves, crushed

1 tablespoon soy sauce

1 tablespoon red chilli sauce

½ tablespoon vinegar

½ teaspoon dried thyme

salt to taste

8-10 black peppercorns, crushed

7-8 fresh basil leaves, roughly torn

Method

1. If using porcini and oyster mushrooms, soak them in lukewarm water for twenty minutes. Drain. Wash well and set aside.
2. Heat the oil in a large pan. Add the onions and sauté over medium heat till translucent. Add the garlic and stir-fry for a minute.

3. Add the mushrooms and red and yellow capsicums and sauté over high heat for three minutes.
4. Add the soy sauce, chilli sauce and vinegar and sauté for another two minutes.
5. Add the thyme, salt and crushed peppercorns. Remove from heat, stir in the basil and serve hot.

Multi-grain Footlong with Mushroom and Chicken

Ingredients

1 multi-grain long loaf

10-12 medium fresh button mushrooms, sliced

6 slices chicken salami

1 tablespoon oil

salt to taste

8-10 black peppercorns, crushed

2 tablespoons Mayonnaise (see below)

8 lettuce leaves, shredded

¼ cup sliced black olives

1 small onion, sliced

5-6 pickled gherkins, sliced

2 cheese slices

tomato ketchup, as required

mustard sauce, as required

Method

1. Heat the oil in a pan. Add the mushrooms and sauté over high heat for one minute. Add the salt and the crushed peppercorns. Sauté for one minute longer and remove from heat.

2. Slit the bread lengthways without cutting through.

3. Spread the insides with mayonnaise. Cover the bottom half with shredded lettuce.

4. Arrange the sliced black olives, onion and pickled gherkins on the lettuce. Cut the cheese slices into two and place on the toppings. Place the mushrooms and chicken salami on top.
5. Drizzle tomato ketchup and mustard sauce over the filling. Press the top half of the loaf down gently to enclose the filling. Cut into smaller pieces and serve immediately.

Mayonnaise

Place 1 egg yolk, salt to taste, ¼ teaspoon each white pepper powder, mustard powder and sugar and 1 teaspoon vinegar in a clean bowl and mix thoroughly with a whisk. Alternatively, process the mixture in a blender. Add 1 cup of oil, a little at a time, whisking or blending continuously, until all the oil is incorporated. Add 1 teaspoon lemon juice and adjust seasoning. Store in an airtight jar in a refrigerator.

Mushroom Quiche

Ingredients

Pastry Crust

1 recipe Basic Shortcrust Pastry (see below)

Filling

225 grams fresh button mushrooms, thinly sliced

1 tablespoon olive oil

½ tablespoon butter

1 garlic clove, crushed

½ tablespoon lemon juice

salt to taste

black pepper powder to taste

1 tablespoon fresh coriander, finely chopped

2 eggs

¾ cup fresh cream

¼ cup grated processed cheese

Method

1. Preheat an oven to 190°C/375°F/Gas Mark 5.
2. Roll out the shortcrust pastry dough into a quarter-inch thick round and line a nine-inch round tart tin with it. Trim the edges and prick the base all over with a fork.
3. For the filling, heat the olive oil and butter in a pan over medium heat; stir in the mushrooms, garlic and lemon juice. Add the salt and pepper powder

and cook until the mushrooms dry out. Increase the heat and cook until the mixture is dry. Add the fresh coriander and adjust seasoning.

4. Whisk the eggs and cream together and stir in the mushroom mixture. Sprinkle the cheese over the base of the tart and pour the mushroom filling over it.
5. Bake in the preheated oven for about thirty-five minutes, or until puffed up and golden brown. Cut into wedges and serve warm. Makes one 9-inch quiche.

Basic Shortcrust Pastry

Process 1 cup refined flour and 60 grams chilled and chopped butter in a food processor until the mixture resembles coarse breadcrumbs. If mixing by hand, rub the butter into the flour with your fingertips.

With the processor running, add drops of iced water until the dough comes together or mix it in with a knife or a wooden spoon or lightly with your fingers. It will need approximately two-and-a-half tablespoons of water.

Press the dough into a ball, wrap in greaseproof paper or cling film and refrigerate for at least thirty minutes before rolling or shaping. Makes enough for one 9-inch pastry base.

Shortcrust pastry can be stored in a refrigerator for two days, or in a freezer for up to three months.

Kaju Khumb Makhana

Ingredients

1 cup whole cashew nuts, soaked

500 grams fresh button mushrooms

2 cups puffed lotus seeds

oil for shallow-frying

½ cup yogurt

1 tablespoon coriander powder

1½ teaspoons red chilli powder

1 teaspoon turmeric powder

2 tablespoons pure ghee

1 teaspoon cumin seeds

3 medium onions, chopped

2 teaspoons ginger paste

2 teaspoons garlic paste

2 teaspoons black pepper powder

1½ cups fresh tomato purée

salt to taste

1 teaspoon *garam masala* powder

1 tablespoon honey (optional)

1 tablespoon lemon juice

2 tablespoons chopped fresh coriander

Method

1. Remove the stalks of the mushrooms, clean and boil until three-fourth cooked. Drain and set aside.

Kaju Khumb Makhana

2. Heat the oil in a *kadai* and shallow-fry the lotus seeds for half a minute. Drain and soak in a bowl of water.
3. Place the yogurt in a bowl; add the coriander powder, chilli powder and turmeric powder and whisk well to mix.
4. Heat the ghee in a pan; add the cumin seeds and when they begin to change colour, add the onions and sauté until translucent. Add the ginger paste and garlic paste and sauté for five minutes. Add the pepper powder and sauté for two minutes. Add the mushrooms and continue to sauté for five minutes. Add the yogurt mixture and cook till the oil separates.
5. Add the tomato purée and salt and sauté till the oil separates again. Add two-and-a-half cups of water and bring to a boil; lower heat and add the cashew nuts and lotus seeds. Cover and simmer, stirring occasionally, for eight to ten minutes.
6. Sprinkle the *garam masala* powder and mix. Stir in the honey and lemon juice. Garnish with fresh coriander and serve with *roti*.

Gobhi Mushroom Chilli Fry

Ingredients

1 medium cauliflower, separated into medium florets

10-12 medium fresh button mushrooms, quartered

8-10 green chillies, chopped

2 spring onions with greens

3 tablespoons cornflour

2 tablespoons soy sauce

salt to taste

1 tablespoon oil + for deep-frying

10 garlic cloves, finely chopped

1 teaspoon white pepper powder

a pinch of MSG

Method

1. Chop the spring onions finely. Chop the greens and reserve for garnishing.
2. Mix together the cornflour, half the soy sauce, salt and green chillies and prepare a thick batter using water as required.
3. Heat plenty of oil in a *kadai*. Dip the cauliflower florets in the batter and deep-fry till golden brown. Drain on absorbent paper and set aside. Keep the remaining batter aside.
4. Heat one tablespoon of oil in a pan and sauté the spring onions. Add the garlic

and continue to sauté on high heat till translucent. Add the mushrooms and cook. Since mushrooms shrink on cooking, take care not to overcook them.

5. Add the remaining soy sauce, fried cauliflower, salt, white pepper powder and MSG.
6. Add the remaining batter and cook till thick.
7. Serve hot, garnished with the spring onion greens.

Rice with Stewed Mushrooms and Chicken

Ingredients

3 cups cooked rice

10 fresh button mushrooms, quartered

¾ cup cooked shredded, boneless chicken

1½ tablespoons light soy sauce

¼ teaspoon MSG (optional)

2 teaspoons wine or sherry (optional)

½ teaspoon black pepper powder

salt to taste

2 tablespoons oil

2 spring onions, chopped

5-6 garlic cloves, chopped

1 inch ginger, chopped

1 cup Chicken Stock (see below)

2 teaspoons cornflour

1 egg omelette, cut into strips

Method

1. Combine the mushrooms and chicken in a bowl. Add the soy sauce, MSG, wine, pepper powder and salt and mix well.
2. Heat the oil in a pan and sauté the spring onions, garlic and ginger till lightly browned.
3. Add the chicken and mushroom mixture and stir-fry for one minute.

4. Add the chicken stock and bring to a boil. Add the cornflour mixed with two tablespoons of water, and stir till the sauce thickens.
5. Arrange the rice on a serving dish and pour the gravy over it.
6. Garnish with the omelette strips and serve hot.

Chicken Stock

Boil 200 grams chicken bones in water for 5 minutes. Drain and discard water. Boil blanched bones with a roughly chopped carrot, celery stalk, leek, 2-3 parsley stalks, 6-7 black peppercorns, 5-6 cloves, 1 bay leaf and 10 cups of water.

Remove any scum which rises to the surface and replace it with more cold water. Simmer for at least one hour.

Remove from heat, strain, cool and store in a refrigerator till further use.

Spinach and Mushroom Risotto

Ingredients

½ bunch (125 grams) spinach, roughly chopped

4-5 fresh button mushrooms, sliced

1½ cups parboiled rice

5 tablespoons butter

1 medium onion, chopped

4-5 garlic cloves, chopped

1 cup white wine

3½ cups Vegetable Stock (page 10) or water

salt to taste

¾ cup grated Parmesan cheese

½ teaspoon pepper powder

½ cup fresh cream

Method

1. Wash and soak the rice for two hours. Drain.
2. Mix together three tablespoons of butter, onion, garlic and mushrooms in a deep microwave-safe dish. Cook, uncovered, on HIGH (100%) for three minutes.
3. Add the rice, wine, half the stock and salt and cook on HIGH (100%) for ten minutes.
4. Stir in the remaining stock and cook on HIGH (100%) for another ten minutes.
5. Stir in the spinach, cheese, pepper powder and cream and mix well. Cook,

uncovered, on HIGH (100%) for two minutes.

6. Mix in the remaining two tablespoons of butter and serve hot.

Chef's Tip

This is a speedy version of the original recipe. Traditionally risotto is made with arborio rice and cooked over low heat, and the stock is added little by little.

Mushroom Dum Biryani

Ingredients

15-20 medium fresh button mushrooms, quartered
1½ cups Basmati rice
1 inch ginger
5 garlic cloves
a generous pinch of saffron
¼ cup skimmed milk, warmed
1 bay leaf
4 cloves
2 green cardamoms
2 black cardamoms
1 inch cinnamon
1 blade mace
salt to taste
2 teaspoons oil
2 medium onions, sliced finely
2 teaspoons red chilli powder
1 tablespoon coriander powder
½ tablespoon crushed peppercorn
½ teaspoon cumin powder
½ teaspoon turmeric powder
2 medium tomatoes, puréed
½ cup skimmed milk yogurt, whisked
½ teaspoon *garam masala* powder
¼ cup fresh coriander, finely chopped
¼ cup fresh mint, finely chopped
4-5 drops *kewra* water (optional)

Mushroom Dum Biryani

Method

1. Soak the rice in sufficient water for half an hour. Drain.
2. Grind together the ginger and garlic to a fine paste. Soak the saffron in the warm milk.
3. Boil three to four cups of water in a thick bottomed vessel; add the bay leaf, cloves, green cardamoms, black cardamoms, cinnamon, mace and one teaspoon salt. When the water starts boiling, add the Basmati rice.
4. Cook for eight to ten minutes, stirring frequently or until the rice is three-fourth done. Drain in a colander.
5. Heat the oil in a non stick pan, add the sliced onions and stir-fry over high heat for two to three minutes or until the onions turns translucent. Add the ginger-garlic paste and cook briefly.
6. Add the chilli powder, coriander powder, crushed peppercorn, cumin powder and turmeric powder. Stir-fry briefly and add the puréed tomatoes.
7. Continue cooking over high heat for another two to three minutes, stirring continuously or until the *masala* is fairly thick.

8. Add the yogurt, *garam masala* powder and half the quantity of chopped fresh coriander and mint. Stir well and cook for two minutes more.
9. Add the quartered button mushrooms and salt to taste. Stir-fry over high heat for two to three minutes and remove from heat.
10. Arrange the cooked rice and mushroom *masala* in alternate layers in an ovenproof dish (or *biryani handi*), sprinkling the chopped fresh coriander and mint, *kewra* water and the saffron-flavoured milk. Ensure that the topmost layer is rice.
11. Cover the assembled *biryani* with a tight fitting lid and seal the edges with *atta* dough (if required).
12. Keep the sealed dish on a medium hot *tawa* and leave for ten to fifteen minutes. You can also place a few burning charcoals on the lid. Alternately, leave the sealed dish in a pre-heated oven for ten to fifteen minutes.
13. Break the seal and open the dish, just before serving.

Mushroom Pot Rice

Ingredients

3-4 oyster mushrooms

10-12 fresh button mushrooms, sliced

1 cup rice, soaked

1 star anise

2 tablespoons cornflour

4 tablespoons oil

1 inch ginger, grated

2-3 garlic cloves, chopped

2 spring onions, chopped

2 tablespoons soy sauce

¼ teaspoon MSG (optional)

½ teaspoon white pepper powder

salt to taste

2 cups Vegetable Stock (page 10)

2 spring onion greens, for garnishing

Method

1. Boil the rice in three cups of water with the star anise until just cooked. Drain well, transfer to a clay pot and keep warm.
2. Soak the oyster mushrooms in hot water for fifteen minutes, drain and chop roughly. Mix the cornflour and half a cup of water. Set aside.
3. Preheat an oven to 180ºC/350ºF/Gas Mark 4.

Mushroom Pot Rice

4. Heat the oil in a wok; add the ginger and garlic and stir-fry for half a minute. Add the spring onions and continue to stir-fry for a minute.
5. Add the soy sauce, oyster mushrooms, MSG, white pepper powder, salt to taste and vegetable stock. Bring to a boil, add the button mushrooms and stir in the cornflour mixture.
6. Cook for a minute or until the sauce thickens, stirring continuously. Pour the sauce over the rice, cover with a lid and cook in the preheated oven for twelve to fifteen minutes.
7. Uncover the pot, stir the contents well, garnish with the spring onion greens and serve hot.

Chilli and Mushroom Fried Rice

Ingredients

4 green chillies, finely chopped

1½ cups sliced fresh button mushrooms

1½ cups cooked rice

3 tablespoons oil

1 inch ginger, finely chopped

6-8 garlic cloves, chopped

5-6 spring onions, finely chopped

a pinch of MSG (optional)

½ teaspoon white pepper powder

salt to taste

1 tablespoon soy sauce

3-4 spring onion greens, finely chopped

Method

1. Heat the oil in a wok; add the ginger, garlic and green chillies and stir-fry for two minutes. Add the spring onions, mushrooms, MSG, white pepper powder and salt, and stir-fry over high heat for two minutes.
2. Add the rice, soy sauce and spring onion greens. Stir-fry over high heat for three minutes.
3. Serve hot.

Herbed Rice with Mushrooms

Ingredients

1 teaspoon dried oregano

1½ cups brown rice

6-7 medium fresh button mushrooms, halved

2 tablespoons olive oil

2 medium onions, chopped

2-3 garlic cloves, chopped

1 inch celery stalk, chopped

salt to taste

Method

1. Soak the brown rice in four or five cups of water for one hour. Drain.
2. Heat the oil in a pressure cooker. Add the onions, garlic and celery and sauté till translucent.
3. Add the drained rice and salt and sauté for one or two minutes. Add three and three-fourth cups of water and bring to a boil.
4. Stir in the mushrooms and bring to a boil again. Seal the cooker with the lid and cook till the pressure is released three times (three whistles).
5. Remove the lid once the pressure has reduced completely. Add the dried oregano and mix. Serve hot.

Tomato and Black Mushroom Risotto

Ingredients

3 medium tomatoes, blanched and finely chopped

8-10 cherry tomatoes

10-12 black mushrooms

1½ cups rice, preferably Arborio

1 tablespoon butter

¼ cup white wine

2 cups Vegetable Stock (page 10)

1 cup skimmed milk

salt to taste

½ teaspoon pepper powder

¼ cup grated low-fat cheese

Method

1. Soak the mushrooms in hot water, drain and roughly chop them.
2. In a thick-bottomed pan, heat half of the butter on medium heat and add the chopped tomatoes. Sauté till they are cooked.
3. Add the chopped mushrooms and stir-fry. Add the Arborio rice and sauté for three to four minutes. Add white wine and cook on high heat for a couple of minutes, stirring frequently.
4. Stir in the stock followed by half the quantity of skimmed milk. Reduce the

heat and cook on medium heat, stirring gently continuously.

5. Cook the rice till it is done, stirring all the time. Season with salt and pepper powder.
6. Just before serving, add the grated cheese and remaining butter and skimmed milk to give it a creamy texture. Top it with cherry tomatoes and serve hot.

Chef's Tip

For making risotto there is no need to soak the rice. The consistency of a risotto is quite thick and lumpy, therefore the rice that you choose should be thick and starchy. If you cannot get Arborio rice or find it too expensive, use rice that you would normally use for khichdi.

Khumb Makai Pulao

Ingredients

20-25 fresh button mushrooms, sliced

¾ cup corn kernels

1½ cups Basmati rice, soaked

1 tablespoon oil

1 teaspoon cumin seeds

1 bay leaf

2 cloves

5 black peppercorns

2 green cardamoms

1 black cardamom

1 inch cinnamon

1 blade mace

1 inch ginger, chopped

2-3 green chillies, slit

salt to taste

1 tablespoon lemon juice

Method

1. Heat the oil in a non-stick pan; add the cumin seeds and when they start to change colour, add the bay leaf, cloves, peppercorns, green cardamoms, black cardamom, cinnamon and mace. Sauté for a few seconds.

2. Add the ginger and green chillies and sauté over medium heat for one minute.

3. Add the corn and mushrooms and continue cooking for two to three minutes. Add the rice, stirring gently for about one minute.
4. Add three cups of water and salt to taste and bring to a boil.
5. Cover and cook over medium heat until the water has almost been absorbed and the rice is cooked. Add the lemon juice and mix gently.
6. Serve hot.

GLOSSARY

ENGLISH	HINDI
Apple	saeb
Baby potatoes	chhote aloo
Bay leaf	tej patta
Beetroot	chukandar
Black cardamoms	badi elaichi
Black peppercorns	kali mirch
Black salt	kala namak
Breadcrumbs	bread ka choora
Butter	makhkhan
Cabbage	pattagobhi
Capsicum	Shimla mirch
Carom seeds	ajwain
Carrots	gajar
Cashew nuts	kaju
Cherry tomatoes	chhote tamatar
Cinnamon	dalchini
Cloves	laung

ENGLISH	HINDI
Cottage cheese	paneer
Cream (dairy)	malai
Cucumber	kakdi/kheera
Cumin seeds	jeera
Dried red chillies	sookhi lal mirch
Egg	anda
Fresh basil leaves	tulsi ki pattiyan
Fresh coriander leaves	hara dhania
Fresh mint leaves	pudine ki tazi pattiyan
Fresh spinach leaves	palak ke taze patte
Garlic cloves	lehsun ki kaliyan
Gram flour	besan
Green cardamoms	chhoti elaichi
Green peas	matar
Honey	shahad/madhu
Iceberg lettuce	salad ke patte

ENGLISH	HINDI
Indian gooseberry	amla
Mace	javitri
Mushrooms	kukurmutta/gucchi/ dhingri/khumb
Mustard	rai
Nutmeg	jaiphal
Olive	jaitun
Parboiled rice	ukda chawal
Poppy seeds	khuskhus
Prunes	sookhe adu
Puffed lotus seeds	makhane
Refined flour	maida
Saffron	kesar
Sesame	til
Skimmed milk	bina malai ka doodh
Spring onion	hara pyaaz
Spring onion greens	hare pyaaz ki pattiyan
Star anise	chakri phool/ badiyan
Sweetcorn kernels	makai ke dane
Tomato purée	pise hue tamatar
Tomatoes	tamatar
Turmeric powder	haldi powder
Unripe bananas	kachche kele
Vermicelli	semiyan
Vinegar	sirka
White pepper	safed mirch
Yogurt	dahi